Thunder & Rain

I. Gagee Johnson

BookLeaf Publishing

India | USA | UK

Thunder & Rain

© 2021 I. Gagee Johnson

I. Gagee Johnson asserts the moral right to be
identified as author of this work.

Presentation by *BookLeaf Publishing*

Web: www.bookleafpub.com

E-mail: info@bookleafpub.com

ISBN: 9789358362275

First Edition 2021

I would like to dedicate this small collection to my Mother. No one has ever understood, loved or believed in me as much as you. I was meant to find you. I want to be just like you one day.

May we both find our peace.

Acknowledgement

Masi Cho to my family whether chosen, found, or born into; I am blessed to be loved by you. A special thank you to my parents and grandparents for their continued love and support.

If you have ever loved or lost, this book is for you. You will find yourself again.

Wisdom

With the knowledge of Seven Generations

prior to myself,

I am dedicated to educating our young

people,

So that the Four Directions we walk in may

stretch beyond the horizons evermore,

Doing what the Creator had envisioned for

me and sharing my gifts,

On my way to joining my Ancestors and

dancing across the sky,

My role is to leave a path youth will choose

to follow.

Safety

Dusty cyan curtains

The twilight slowly fades

My heart by my side

Chains and Bands

A promise, a commitment and a gift out of
love,

Three hearts never to be the same,

They still remain tangled and hidden away

Nookwez *(Smudge)*

Great Spirit, hear my prayers

May smoke lead them to the Eagle

So they may reach You

2:37

Another day of hustle and bustle has come
and gone

Now there is quiet as the townspeople sleep,
as if the city is waiting anxiously for the
new day to be set in motion

The roads are bare as dust settles upon the
boardwalk

The wind whistling over the hills is the only
sound

The house is still as the faint glow of the
twinkle lights softly tiptoe down the stairs
and slip beneath the door

In the darkest corner of the room

Near a drafty window

The curtain is a shield, blocking out the
summer sun that never ceases

The deafening silence rings in my ears

It beckons me so, coaxing my mind to fill
the night with distraction

Music, art, a lover, anything

Those thoughts that I carefully packed away
in a shoebox, buried in the closet of my
mind

They race, flooding my every sense with
feelings I had forgotten

Like a siren, they are all consuming

Doubt creeps into my heart

Old memories force themselves to the
surface of the ocean that is my imagination

But what truly keeps me up at this hour
more than anything else is love.

The love I have given, and that I have
received

The love I've lost, and the love that had to
leave

The question I always come back to is this

Where does love begin and where does it
end?

For me, love is like an old friend

When they come to visit you invite them in
and embrace them warmly

As they depart, sadness is inevitable

Love says farewell, and while it feels like
goodbye forever

I know in my heart that it will return.

Conquering The Day

Today

When all wanted to do was lay in bed

I got up.

I fought for my joy

I washed myself of the doubts lingering
from the early hours of the morning

Today my favourite shirt was battle armor

My jeans are stilts, lifting my spirits in the
air

I put on my eyeliner like it is war paint

My highlighter transforms me into a strong,
melanated goddess

My boots, command respect with every step
I take

I keep my medicines close to my heart for
balance and peace

I adorn myself with perfume, it enhances my
magic, it instills awe in all who cross my
path

I fix my hair, it is fierce and holds all my
knowledge

My pocket knife holstered at my hip is my
sword of protection

Today the sad will lose. I am ready.

Shelter

I've been up all night counting the lies he told me

Daydreaming of the sweetness in his voice as the poison escaped his lips

I would drink it in willingly if he had asked me, without question

But he never really asked, his venom just seeped into every part of the life we had built

And in a time when I was trying to establish who I was, and who I wanted to be

He had soured my mind to forget all I was worthy of, unbeknownst to me

Now that years have passed, I have
discovered my true self

But still some nights I think of where I
might be if I just let it turn me into clay

Easily molded by his carefully placed hands

Never knowing what form I could truly take
if given the chance

I remember my awakening

All at once I became painfully aware that
my own lover had twisted my mind to
accept the unacceptable

His voice was like thunder that day, a roar of
anger and an unstoppable force

The lightning in his eyes revealed a warning
to me

And just like that I knew I could not be

caught in his storm for a second longer

That day I left him on his porch,

I built a shelter in anticipation of the

downpour,

It never came.

Every now and then, there is thunder

And I can feel shaking of the ground I stand

upon

However now that I have my strength back

It will require more than just poison, to take

me out.

In Another Life

In another life, I know we were in love,

Because of the way you held me with the
Aurora dancing above,

I'm not sure how we met, if we married, if
you left,

But in another life we were in love.

Maybe we were like two ships passing in the
night, an almost, but never getting it right

Maybe we grew old together, side by side
until the end,

Or maybe we were Otters floating on the
river, fast asleep and holding hands.

Regardless of who we were, how we were
and when,

I believe all this déja vu, that familiarity of you, is because we've been here before.

One thing is for certain, in this life I plan to love you more.

Lighthouse

The Creator knew I was meant to be yours before we ever met,

I believe I needed you more than words can express, and still do in some ways.

When I was a child, you took care of me.

The memories and lessons helped shape the way I move on this world. You were my teacher.

When I grew older, I felt as if I was lost at Sea, always trying to stay afloat when the hope of a better day seemed impossible,

You became my Lighthouse, a glowing stream guiding me to calmer waters.

You gave me all it could ever want in this life, a home.

Somewhere I can always come back to,

A safe haven, where love fills every room
and I long for nothing.

Now that I am a young woman, you have
taken on a new role, as my most trusted
elder in the community I've built.

I am blessed to have your wise counsel and I
often turn to you in times of uncertainty,

For you always seem to know just what to
do

You are unafraid to be brutally honest, and
tell me if I am straying from the Red Road.

Along with the wisdom and teachings you
have given me, our time together is the part
of us that brings me the most joy.

When I am off on one of my adventures, and
missing you and our home,

I reflect on those summer evenings,

You and mom and I, three generations of
remarkable women,

Sipping wine, telling stories, reminiscing,
and the laughter we all share.

If I close my eyes, I can still smell the
sweetness of the wildflowers in the air,

I can hear the hum of Crickets and Frogs,
and the distant howling of the Coywolves.

Sitting beneath the porch light, in our little
corner of the universe, looking at the stars
and taking in the warmth of the night.

We have a balance you see; I help you with
the things you can no longer do with the
ease you did in your youth,

And you help me learn all that I will need to
know and pass on to future generations.

Please know I carry you close to my heart in all that I do, and wherever I go,

And remember that I love you more than the Dove loves serenading the sunrise.

For all you are, were and are yet to be, I am just glad to call you mine.

Patience

The candlelight dances on the walls,
illuminating the room.

Reflecting in half full glasses, creating the
illusion of fire within the wine.

The pitter-patter of little feet, long ago
silenced by peaceful dreams and restful
sleep.

The house is filled with the hushed words
and the soft strumming of a six string

Medicine floats through the air, the melodies
from the heart, healing as each note rings
out.

The beating of two hearts in sync as the
song goes on.

There is a serenity that echoes through the space.

Their skin is golden, like honey, they feel as pure as the nectar of the gods.

Eyes that in the sobriety of day tell a story of dispiriting past lives, now have acclimated to the darkness of the early hours of the morning.

The tenebrous burnt umber tinted irises, regard me in such a way that I have never seen. Peering into the depths of my mind.

By night these transform from mere vision aids to windows of the soul.

The music stops as a gentle hand caresses my cheek and finds its final resting place.

Carefully petting my knee, the benevolence replenishes the parts of me I thought would

forever be hollowed by my vituperative past
lovers.

We are only in this moment, basking in the
glow of a newfound love.

The ancestors have been praying for
moments like these.

It Begins With One

We could change the world, just you and I,

by loving one another.

Where all I'd ever need, is you holding me.

I can't imagine a better way, for life with

you to ever be.

Loss

In the embrace of a young child, with that smile that could light up the darkest of nights. Wind swept hair the colour of bleached sand, and eyes as blue as sea. A laugh so cheerful and carefree, a deaf man smiles. Never again will I be in the presence of this magic. Only occurring once in a lifetime and it has changed me and shifted my previous belief on the truth of this existence. When I imagine your final thoughts, I pray they were of the sun and fields of joy. Perhaps they were dark as you helplessly submitted to another fate. Only you will ever know my darling, with the light that shines no more. Remember all you left behind.

A Carriage of Love

My father's car was a deep green, just like
the pines outside of 163. It was warm inside
from the heat of the day. It always smelt of
his cologne. The velvety interior, brushing
against my skin. I imagine I am on a throne.
I sit raised in the center of the backseat.
Listening to all the songs we wrote together.
I watch the scenes change as we drive on.
As the sun begins to meet the horizon and
the streetlights awaken from their slumber.
The soft light of the evening streams into my
window as this becomes my traveling
cradle.

Lights illuminate our path, take us home
safely.

RED

Red is bold

Red is brave

Red is strong

Red is timeless

The suffering will end.

Red is love

Red is confident

Red is honest

Red is pain

Suffer no more.

Red is kind

Red is wise

Red is beautiful

Red is powerful

This is my new beginning.

I am Red.

REMEMBER ME WELL

The journey of healing I must embark upon,

Starts with leaving you,

And even though my heart is breaking,

I know this much is true.

I gave you all I had to give,

And the best that I could be,

You said you would return a man,

I doubtfully responded "we'll see".

I do not wish to say goodbye,

Or turn and walk away,

Sometimes forever isn't that long,

But at least we have today.

Remember me well.

Impromptu Visit I

As your closing remarks of self defense rang
in my ears,

Echoing through my veins, ensuring every
fingertip and hair on my head knew,

My heart stopped

I drew my final breath as myself

I held it in, I stopped everything

I did not speak, I did not move, I did not cry

The survivor in me took control of this
vessel,

And like you would a child, She shielded me
from the inevitable pain

She took me away from the wreckage

I took Her hand and we disappeared

I never know where we go when She takes me and She gives me no say on when I return.

I look over my shoulder to see my body, exactly where I left it,

Sitting on the couch, starting intensely at a wrinkle in the leather.

My body doesn't know what to do without me in it, it becomes silent and still, unmoving, it offers no reaction to your attempts to reach me.

I am already gone.

Impromptu Visit II

I do not see what happens next,

But I awaken in my bed to the light of a new
day

With a dull aching beneath my breast.

My body lay there, awaiting my return

She is taking me home, we walk slowly

across a desert of disorientation

I am not quite myself in this moment,
something is different,

The place is barren and there is a
nothingness that is disguised as calm.

She places me back into my consciousness,
giving me a kiss before she departs,
reminding me that she will protect me
always,

That She knows best, She fades into the
darkest corner of my mind where She
resides when I don't need Her

 Once I am alone again, the realization
begins

Slowly then all at once, beginning as a
droplet or two of mist running down the
window pane

And then the skies open up and release their
entirety, they cloud my thoughts and block
the sun

Thoughts make attempts to blossom into
sentences;

Like a lotus fighting through the muddied
waters to reach the surface,

But there is no avail, the clenching of my
jaw holds them in my mouth until they die
and decompose into the saliva.

I open my mouth but there are no words.

There is a whisper of a memory in my heart,

The words, the ones that had called Her
forward, were an unspoken invitation.

Everytime I hear them, She visits me. Right
on cue, insisting that we leave the mess of a
broken heart and a wounded spirit behind.

We never take my body with us, It would
only weigh us down She tells me

We abandon my body, now comatose.

We just float upwards,

To the ceiling, through the roof until the sky
is all we have,

We surpass the constellations and planets,

and then there is just Her and I.

Together in the quiet.

The End Of The Tunnel

A poisoned mind is a dangerous place

Where sadness paints the walls

The roads are paved with indignation

Immersed in memories one cannot erase

Above the skies are filled with regret

Down below, the earth swells with guilt

In through the darkness the demons doth
creep

Yet sunrise comes after sunset

The Spark of a Taboo Love

With Vodka rushing through our veins,

You dare to take a chance

Music pulses in the air, covering a hushed
conversation

You grab my hand and pull me close,

Pressed together, swaying in unison

I am utterly aware of the proximity,

Our foreheads meeting, eyes closed

Because the best things in life you don't see,
you feel

Hearts pounding with the question of more

But as the song ends, and I pull away

My smile matches yours

The dance is over, yet your hand never leaves mine.

The Loudest Silence

By the cloak of darkness, beneath that
golden harvest moon,

The cool breeze caressed our skin

Our hearts finally slowing as we held each
other tight,

How could it have been so wrong, if it felt
so right?

And as you reminded me of eight letters,
three words,

This is how I wish to remember you and I.

The anticipation of the near touch, an
almost,

Laying in the bed of your truck, regarding
the breathtaking ocean of stars above,

And fighting the butterflies within.

A dance by the fireside I was too far gone to
recall,

But a smile I will never forget.

The way we locked eyes in the bar room,

A mic in your hand, a drink in mine,

The nights we watched the sun set upon the
bay,

Or the way my hand felt when it found
yours, like nothing fit until you,

Tonight changed all of this. But if we walk
away, knowing what we know and feeling
how we felt,

Enjoy the sound of my silence, as I gently close the door.

Little Flower

My love for you is everlasting

It will out live us both

It has weathered the ever changing tides

It is loyal, like the Wolf to the Pack

When the Sun is shining on us, we will
smile at the sky

And when the Mountain's are crashing down
around you

I will be your shield, I will keep you safe.

You are braver than you know

Like Flora emerging from the ashes.

You are my cheerleader, foam finger in hand

Thank you for believing in me.

I am with you always,

You are my heart.

9 789358 362275